If Lost, Please Return This Planner To:

_____

_____

2020 At A Glance

January

S	M	T	W	T	F	S
			1	2	3	4
5	6	7	8	9	10	11
12	13	14	15	16	17	18
19	20	21	22	23	24	25
26	27	28	29	30	31	

February

S	M	T	W	T	F	S
						1
2	3	4	5	6	7	8
9	10	11	12	13	14	15
16	17	18	19	20	21	22
23	24	25	26	27	28	29

March

S	M	T	W	T	F	S
1	2	3	4	5	6	7
8	9	10	11	12	13	14
15	16	17	18	19	20	21
22	23	24	25	26	27	28
29	30	31				

April

S	M	T	W	T	F	S
			1	2	3	4
5	6	7	8	9	10	11
12	13	14	15	16	17	18
19	20	21	22	23	24	25
26	27	28	29	30		

May

S	M	T	W	T	F	S
					1	2
3	4	5	6	7	8	9
10	11	12	13	14	15	16
17	18	19	20	21	22	23
24	25	26	27	28	29	30
31						

June

S	M	T	W	T	F	S
	1	2	3	4	5	6
7	8	9	10	11	12	13
14	15	16	17	18	19	20
21	22	23	24	25	26	27
28	29	30				

July

S	M	T	W	T	F	S
			1	2	3	4
5	6	7	8	9	10	11
12	13	14	15	16	17	18
19	20	21	22	23	24	25
26	27	28	29	30	31	

August

S	M	T	W	T	F	S
						1
2	3	4	5	6	7	8
9	10	11	12	13	14	15
16	17	18	19	20	21	22
23	24	25	26	27	28	29
30	31					

September

S	M	T	W	T	F	S
		1	2	3	4	5
6	7	8	9	10	11	12
13	14	15	16	17	18	19
20	21	22	23	24	25	26
27	28	29	30			

October

S	M	T	W	T	F	S
				1	2	3
4	5	6	7	8	9	10
11	12	13	14	15	16	17
18	19	20	21	22	23	24
25	26	27	28	29	30	31

November

S	M	T	W	T	F	S
1	2	3	4	5	6	7
8	9	10	11	12	13	14
15	16	17	18	19	20	21
22	23	24	25	26	27	28
29	30					

December

S	M	T	W	T	F	S
		1	2	3	4	5
6	7	8	9	10	11	12
13	14	15	16	17	18	19
20	21	22	23	24	25	26
27	28	29	30	31		

Dog Walking
2020 Planner

Services and Pricing

Dog Walking		
TIME	TYPE	PRICE
15 minute dog Walk	On Leash	$
30 minute dog Walk	On Leash	$
60 minute dog Walk	On Leash	$
15 minute dog Walk	Off Leash	$
Dog Exercising		
15 Minute Run	On Leash	$
20 Minute Run	On Leash	$
15 Minute Run	Off Leash	$
20 Minute Run	Off Leash	$

Client List

Location and Contact Information

Name:

Address:

Phone:

Name:

Address:

Phone:

Name:

Address:

Phone:

Name:

Address:

Phone:

Client List

Location and Contact Information

Name:

Address:

Phone:

Name:

Address:

Phone:

Name:

Address:

Phone:

Name:

Address:

Phone:

Client List

Location and Contact Information

Name:

Address:

Phone:

Name:

Address:

Phone:

Name:

Address:

Phone:

Name:

Address:

Phone:

Client List

Location and Contact Information

Name:

Address:

Phone:

Name:

Address:

Phone:

Name:

Address:

Phone:

Name:

Address:

Phone:

Client Agreed Services

Client Name: _____

Start date: _____

Payment Information Amount -	❑ CC ❑ Cash ❑ Cheque ❑ Other	_____ _____ _____ _____	Due ❑ On Delivery ❑ Weekly ❑ Monthly

Pet Details	Breed	Temperament	Name

Service Type	Time	Schedule	
Walk			
Run			
Off Leash			

Notes:

Client Agreed Services

Client Name: _____

Start date: _____

Payment Information Amount -	☐ CC ☐ Cash ☐ Cheque ☐ Other	_____ _____ _____ _____	Due ☐ On Delivery ☐ Weekly ☐ Monthly

Pet Details	Breed	Temperament	Name

Service Type	Time	Schedule
Walk		
Run		
Off Leash		

Notes:

_____

_____

_____

_____

_____

Client Agreed Services

Client Name: _____

Start date: _____

Payment Information Amount -	❏ CC ❏ Cash ❏ Cheque ❏ Other	_____ _____ _____ _____	Due ❏ On Delivery ❏ Weekly ❏ Monthly

Pet Details	Breed	Temperament	Name

Service Type	Time	Schedule	
Walk			
Run			
Off Leash			

Notes:

Client Agreed Services

Client Name: _____

Start date: _____

Payment Information Amount -	☐ CC ☐ Cash ☐ Cheque ☐ Other	_____ _____ _____ _____	Due ☐ On Delivery ☐ Weekly ☐ Monthly

Pet Details	Breed	Temperament	Name

Service Type	Time	Schedule	
Walk			
Run			
Off Leash			

Notes:

_____

_____

_____

_____

_____

Client Agreed Services

Client Name: _____

Start date: _____

Payment Information Amount -	❑ CC ❑ Cash ❑ Cheque ❑ Other	_____ _____ _____ _____	Due ❑ On Delivery ❑ Weekly ❑ Monthly

Pet Details	Breed	Temperament	Name

Service Type	Time	Schedule	
Walk			
Run			
Off Leash			

Notes:

_____

_____

_____

_____

_____

Client Agreed Services

Client Name: _____

Start date: _____

Payment Information Amount -	❏ CC ❏ Cash ❏ Cheque ❏ Other	_____ _____ _____ _____	Due ❏ On Delivery ❏ Weekly ❏ Monthly

Pet Details	Breed	Temperament	Name

Service Type	Time	Schedule	
Walk			
Run			
Off Leash			

Notes:

_____

_____

_____

_____

_____

Client Agreed Services

Client Name: _____

Start date: _____

Payment Information Amount -	☐ CC ☐ Cash ☐ Cheque ☐ Other	_____ _____ _____ _____	Due ☐ On Delivery ☐ Weekly ☐ Monthly

Pet Details	Breed	Temperament	Name

Service Type	Time	Schedule	
Walk			
Run			
Off Leash			

Notes:

Client Agreed Services

Client Name: _____

Start date: _____

Payment Information Amount -	❑ CC ❑ Cash ❑ Cheque ❑ Other	_____ _____ _____ _____	Due ❑ On Delivery ❑ Weekly ❑ Monthly

Pet Details	Breed	Temperament	Name

Service Type	Time	Schedule	
Walk			
Run			
Off Leash			

Notes:
_____

_____

_____

_____

_____

_____

Off Leash Parks

Park Name	Location	Hours

Happiness is a
warm puppy

Dog Friendly Parks

Park Name	Location	Hours

Dogs

Breed	Name	Specific Needs

January 1-4

This Week

1   Wednesday

2   Thursday

3   Friday

4   Saturday

January 5-11

This Week

5 Sunday

6 Monday

7 Tuesday

8 Wednesday

9 Thursday

10 Friday

11 Saturday

Notes

top priorities for this week

_____
_____
_____
_____
_____

Victories for the week

looking ahead to next week

_____
_____
_____
_____
_____
_____
_____

January 12-18

This Week

12 Sunday

13 Monday

14 Tuesday

15 Wednesday

16 Thursday

17 Friday

18 Saturday

Notes

top priorities for this week

_____
_____
_____
_____
_____

Victories for the week

looking ahead to next week

_____
_____
_____
_____
_____
_____
_____

January 19-25

This Week

19 Sunday

20 Monday

21 Tuesday

22 Wednesday

23 Thursday

24 Friday

25 Saturday

Notes

top priorities for this week

_____
_____
_____
_____
_____

Victories for the week

looking ahead to next week

_____
_____
_____
_____
_____
_____
_____
_____

January 26-February 1

This Week

26 Sunday

27 Monday

28 Tuesday

29 Wednesday

30 Thursday

31 Friday

Saturday

Notes

top priorities for this week

_____
_____
_____
_____
_____

Victories for the week

looking ahead to next week

_____
_____
_____
_____
_____
_____
_____
_____

February 2-8

This Week

---

2 Sunday

3 Monday

4 Tuesday

5 Wednesday

Thursday

top priorities for this week

_____
_____
_____
_____
_____

Friday

Victories for the week

Saturday

looking ahead to next week

_____
_____
_____
_____
_____
_____
_____
_____

Notes

February 9-15

This Week

9 Sunday

10 Monday

11 Tuesday

12 Wednesday

13 Thursday

top priorities for this week

_____

_____

_____

_____

_____

14 Friday

Victories for the week

15 Saturday

looking ahead to next week

_____

_____

_____

_____

_____

_____

_____

_____

Notes

February 16-22

This Week

16 Sunday

17 Monday

18 Tuesday

19 Wednesday

20 Thursday

21 Friday

22 Saturday

Notes

top priorities for this week

_____
_____
_____
_____
_____

Victories for the week

looking ahead to next week

_____
_____
_____
_____
_____
_____
_____
_____

February 23-29

This Week

23 Sunday

24 Monday

25 Tuesday

26 Wednesday

27 Thursday

28 Friday

29 Saturday

Notes

top priorities for this week

_____
_____
_____
_____
_____

Victories for the week

looking ahead to next week

_____
_____
_____
_____
_____
_____
_____
_____

March 1-7

This Week

1 Sunday

2 Monday

3 Tuesday

4 Wednesday

5 Thursday

6 Friday

7 Saturday

Notes

top priorities for this week

_____

_____

_____

_____

_____

Victories for the week

looking ahead to next week

_____

_____

_____

_____

_____

_____

_____

_____

March 8-14

This Week

_____
_____
_____
_____
_____
_____
_____
_____
_____
_____
_____
_____
_____
_____
_____
_____
_____
_____
_____

8 Sunday

9 Monday

10 Tuesday

11 Wednesday

12 Thursday

13 Friday

14 Saturday

Notes

top priorities for this week

_____
_____
_____
_____
_____

Victories for the week

looking ahead to next week

_____
_____
_____
_____
_____
_____
_____
_____

March 15-21

This Week

_____
_____
_____
_____

_____
_____
_____
_____
_____

_____
_____
_____
_____
_____

_____
_____
_____
_____
_____

15 Sunday

16 Monday

17 Tuesday

18 Wednesday

19 Thursday

20 Friday

21 Saturday

Notes

top priorities for this week

_____
_____
_____
_____
_____

Victories for the week

looking ahead to next week

_____
_____
_____
_____
_____
_____
_____
_____

March 22-28

This Week

22 Sunday

23 Monday

24 Tuesday

25 Wednesday

26 Thursday

top priorities for this week
_____
_____
_____
_____
_____

27 Friday

Victories for the week

28 Saturday

looking ahead to next week
_____
_____
_____
_____
_____
_____
_____

Notes

March 29-April 4

This Week

29 Sunday

30 Monday

31 Tuesday

1 Wednesday

2 Thursday

3 Friday

4 Saturday

Notes

top priorities for this week

_____
_____
_____
_____
_____

Victories for the week

looking ahead to next week

_____
_____
_____
_____
_____
_____
_____

April 5-11

This Week

_____
_____
_____
_____
_____
_____
_____
_____
_____
_____
_____
_____
_____
_____
_____
_____
_____
_____
_____
_____

5 Sunday

6 Monday

7 Tuesday

8 Wednesday

9 Thursday

10 Friday

11 Saturday

Notes

top priorities for this week

_____

_____

_____

_____

_____

Victories for the week

looking ahead to next week

_____

_____

_____

_____

_____

_____

_____

April 12-18

This Week

_____

_____

_____

_____

_____

_____

_____

_____

_____

_____

_____

_____

_____

_____

_____

_____

_____

_____

_____

_____

_____

12 Sunday

13 Monday

14 Tuesday

15 Wednesday

16 Thursday

17 Friday

18 Saturday

Notes

top priorities for this week

_____
_____
_____
_____
_____

Victories for the week

looking ahead to next week

_____
_____
_____
_____
_____
_____
_____
_____

April 19-25

This Week

19 Sunday

20 Monday

21 Tuesday

22 Wednesday

23 Thursday

24 Friday

25 Saturday

Notes

top priorities for this week

_____
_____
_____
_____
_____

Victories for the week

looking ahead to next week

_____
_____
_____
_____
_____
_____
_____
_____

April 26-May 2

This Week

26 Sunday

27 Monday

28 Tuesday

29 Wednesday

30 Thursday

Friday

Saturday

Notes

top priorities for this week

_____
_____
_____
_____
_____

Victories for the week

looking ahead to next week

_____
_____
_____
_____
_____
_____
_____
_____

May 3-9

This Week

_____
_____
_____
_____
_____
_____
_____
_____
_____
_____
_____
_____
_____
_____
_____
_____
_____
_____
_____

3 Sunday

4 Monday

5 Tuesday

6 Wednesday

7 Thursday

top priorities for this week

_____

_____

_____

_____

_____

8 Friday

Victories for the week

Saturday

looking ahead to next week

_____

_____

_____

_____

Notes

_____

_____

_____

_____

May 10-16

This Week

10 Sunday

11 Monday

12 Tuesday

13 Wednesday

14 Thursday

15 Friday

16 Saturday

Notes

top priorities for this week

Victories for the week

looking ahead to next week

May 17-23

This Week

_____
_____
_____
_____
_____
_____
_____
_____
_____
_____
_____
_____
_____
_____
_____
_____
_____
_____
_____
_____
_____
_____

17 Sunday

18 Monday

19 Tuesday

20 Wednesday

21 Thursday

22 Friday

23 Saturday

Notes

top priorities for this week

_____
_____
_____
_____
_____

Victories for the week

looking ahead to next week

_____
_____
_____
_____
_____
_____
_____

May 24-30

This Week

24 Sunday

25 Monday

26 Tuesday

27 Wednesday

28 Thursday

29 Friday

30 Saturday

Notes

top priorities for this week

_____

_____

_____

_____

_____

Victories for the week

looking ahead to next week

_____

_____

_____

_____

_____

_____

_____

May 31–June 6

This Week

31 Sunday

1 Monday

2 Tuesday

3 Wednesday

4 Thursday

5 Friday

6 Saturday

Notes

top priorities for this week

_____

_____

_____

_____

_____

Victories for the week

looking ahead to next week

_____

_____

_____

_____

_____

_____

_____

_____

June 7-13

This Week

7 Sunday

8 Monday

9 Tuesday

10 Wednesday

11 Thursday

12 Friday

13 Saturday

Notes

top priorities for this week

Victories for the week

looking ahead to next week

June 14-20

This Week

_____

_____

_____

_____

_____

_____

_____

_____

_____

_____

_____

_____

_____

_____

_____

_____

_____

_____

_____

_____

_____

_____

14 Sunday

15 Monday

16 Tuesday

17 Wednesday

18 Thursday

19 Friday

20 Saturday

Notes

top priorities for this week

_____
_____
_____
_____
_____

Victories for the week

looking ahead to next week

_____
_____
_____
_____
_____
_____
_____

June 21-27

This Week

_____
_____
_____
_____

_____
_____
_____
_____
_____
_____

_____
_____
_____
_____
_____

_____
_____
_____
_____
_____

21 Sunday

22 Monday

23 Tuesday

24 Wednesday

25 Thursday

26 Friday

27 Saturday

Notes

top priorities for this week

_____

_____

_____

_____

_____

Victories for the week

looking ahead to next week

_____

_____

_____

_____

_____

_____

_____

June 28-July 4

This Week

_____

_____

_____

_____

_____

_____

_____

_____

_____

_____

_____

_____

_____

_____

_____

_____

_____

_____

_____

_____

28 Sunday

29 Monday

30 Tuesday

1 Wednesday

2 Thursday

3 Friday

4 Saturday

Notes

top priorities for this week

_____

_____

_____

_____

_____

Victories for the week

looking ahead to next week

_____

_____

_____

_____

_____

_____

_____

_____

July 5-11

This Week

_____
_____
_____
_____
_____
_____
_____
_____
_____
_____
_____
_____
_____
_____
_____
_____
_____
_____
_____
_____

5 Sunday

6 Monday

7 Tuesday

8 Wednesday

9 Thursday

10 Friday

11 Saturday

Notes

top priorities for this week

_____
_____
_____
_____
_____

Victories for the week

looking ahead to next week

_____
_____
_____
_____
_____
_____
_____
_____

July 12-18

This Week

_____
_____
_____
_____
_____
_____
_____
_____
_____
_____
_____
_____
_____
_____
_____
_____
_____
_____
_____
_____
_____
_____

12 Sunday

13 Monday

14 Tuesday

15 Wednesday

16 Thursday

17 Friday

18 Saturday

Notes

top priorities for this week

_____
_____
_____
_____
_____

Victories for the week

looking ahead to next week

_____
_____
_____
_____
_____
_____
_____

July 19-25

This Week

19 Sunday

20 Monday

21 Tuesday

22 Wednesday

23 Thursday

24 Friday

25 Saturday

Notes

_____

_____

_____

_____

_____

Victories for the week

looking ahead to next week

_____

_____

_____

_____

_____

_____

_____

_____

July 26-August 1

This Week

26 Sunday

27 Monday

28 Tuesday

29 Wednesday

30 Thursday

31 Friday

1 Saturday

Notes

top priorities for this week

_____
_____
_____
_____
_____

Victories for the week

looking ahead to next week

_____
_____
_____
_____
_____
_____
_____

August 2-8

This Week

_____
_____
_____
_____
_____
_____
_____
_____
_____
_____
_____
_____
_____
_____
_____
_____
_____
_____
_____
_____
_____

2 Sunday

3 Monday

4 Tuesday

5 Wednesday

6 Thursday

7 Friday

8 Saturday

Notes

top priorities for this week

_____
_____
_____
_____
_____

Victories for the week

---

looking ahead to next week

_____
_____
_____
_____
_____
_____
_____
_____

August 9-15

This Week

9 Sunday

10 Monday

11 Tuesday

12 Wednesday

13 Thursday

14 Friday

15 Saturday

Notes

top priorities for this week

_____
_____
_____
_____
_____

Victories for the week

looking ahead to next week

_____
_____
_____
_____
_____
_____
_____
_____

August 16-22

This Week

16 Sunday

17 Monday

18 Tuesday

19 Wednesday

20 Thursday

21 Friday

22 Saturday

Notes

top priorities for this week

_____

_____

_____

_____

_____

Victories for the week

looking ahead to next week

_____

_____

_____

_____

_____

_____

_____

August 23-29

This Week

---

23 Sunday

24 Monday

25 Tuesday

26 Wednesday

27 Thursday

28 Friday

29 Saturday

Notes

top priorities for this week

_____
_____
_____
_____
_____

Victories for the week

looking ahead to next week

_____
_____
_____
_____
_____
_____
_____

August 30-September 5

This Week

_____

_____

_____

_____

_____

_____

_____

_____

_____

_____

_____

_____

_____

_____

_____

_____

_____

_____

_____

_____

_____

30 Sunday

31 Monday

1 Tuesday

2 Wednesday

3 Thursday

4 Friday

5 Saturday

Notes

top priorities for this week

_____
_____
_____
_____
_____

Victories for the week

looking ahead to next week

_____
_____
_____
_____
_____
_____
_____
_____

September 6-12

This Week

_____

_____

_____

_____

_____

_____

_____

_____

_____

_____

_____

_____

_____

_____

_____

_____

_____

_____

_____

_____

6 Sunday

7 Monday

8 Tuesday

9 Wednesday

10 Thursday

top priorities for this week

_____
_____
_____
_____
_____

11 Friday

Victories for the week

12 Saturday

looking ahead to next week

Notes

_____
_____
_____
_____
_____
_____
_____

September 13-19

This Week

13 Sunday

14 Monday

15 Tuesday

16 Wednesday

17 Thursday

18 Friday

19 Saturday

Notes

top priorities for this week

_____

_____

_____

_____

_____

Victories for the week

looking ahead to next week

_____

_____

_____

_____

_____

_____

_____

_____

September 20-26

This Week

20 Sunday

21 Monday

22 Tuesday

23 Wednesday

24 Thursday

25 Friday

26 Saturday

Notes

top priorities for this week

Victories for the week

looking ahead to next week

September 27-October 3

This Week

27 Sunday

28 Monday

29 Tuesday

30 Wednesday

1 Thursday

2 Friday

3 Saturday

Notes

top priorities for this week

_____
_____
_____
_____
_____

Victories for the week

looking ahead to next week

_____
_____
_____
_____
_____
_____
_____

October 4-10

This Week

4 Sunday

5 Monday

6 Tuesday

7 Wednesday

8 Thursday

9 Friday

10 Saturday

Notes

top priorities for this week

_____
_____
_____
_____
_____

Victories for the week

looking ahead to next week

_____
_____
_____
_____
_____
_____
_____

October 11-17

This Week

11 Sunday

12 Monday

13 Tuesday

14 Wednesday

15 Thursday

16 Friday

17 Saturday

Notes

top priorities for this week

_____

_____

_____

_____

_____

Victories for the week

looking ahead to next week

_____

_____

_____

_____

_____

_____

_____

October 18-24

This Week

18 Sunday

19 Monday

20 Tuesday

21 Wednesday

22 Thursday

23 Friday

24 Saturday

Notes

top priorities for this week

_____
_____
_____
_____
_____

Victories for the week

---

looking ahead to next week

_____
_____
_____
_____
_____
_____
_____

_____

October 25-31

This Week

25 Sunday

26 Monday

27 Tuesday

28 Wednesday

29 Thursday

top priorities for this week
_____
_____
_____
_____
_____

30 Friday

Victories for the week

31 Saturday

looking ahead to next week
_____
_____
_____
_____
_____
_____
_____

Notes

November 1-7

This Week

1 Sunday

2 Monday

3 Tuesday

4 Wednesday

5 Thursday

6 Friday

7 Saturday

Notes

top priorities for this week

_____
_____
_____
_____
_____

Victories for the week

looking ahead to next week

_____
_____
_____
_____
_____
_____
_____

November 8-14

This Week

8 Sunday

9 Monday

10 Tuesday

11 Wednesday

12 Thursday

13 Friday

14 Saturday

Notes

top priorities for this week

_____

_____

_____

_____

_____

Victories for the week

looking ahead to next week

_____

_____

_____

_____

_____

_____

_____

_____

November 15-21

This Week

15 Sunday

16 Monday

17 Tuesday

18 Wednesday

19 Thursday

20 Friday

21 Saturday

Notes

top priorities for this week

_____
_____
_____
_____
_____

Victories for the week

looking ahead to next week

_____
_____
_____
_____
_____
_____
_____

November 22-28

This Week

22 Sunday

23 Monday

24 Tuesday

25 Wednesday

26 Thursday

27 Friday

28 Saturday

Notes

top priorities for this week

_____
_____
_____
_____
_____

```
┌─────────────────────────────┐
│       Victories for the week │
│                             │
│                             │
│                             │
│                             │
│                             │
│                             │
└─────────────────────────────┘
```

looking ahead to next week

_____
_____
_____
_____
_____
_____
_____

November 29-December 5

This Week

29 Sunday

30 Monday

1 Tuesday

2 Wednesday

3 Thursday

4 Friday

5 Saturday

Notes

top priorities for this week

_____

_____

_____

_____

_____

Victories for the week

looking ahead to next week

_____

_____

_____

_____

_____

_____

_____

December 6-12

This Week

6 Sunday

7 Monday

8 Tuesday

9 Wednesday

10 Thursday

11 Friday

12 Saturday

Notes

top priorities for this week

_____
_____
_____
_____
_____

Victories for the week

looking ahead to next week

_____
_____
_____
_____
_____
_____
_____

December 13-19

This Week

13 Sunday

14 Monday

15 Tuesday

16 Wednesday

17 Thursday

18 Friday

19 Saturday

Notes

top priorities for this week

_____

_____

_____

_____

_____

Victories for the week

looking ahead to next week

_____

_____

_____

_____

_____

_____

_____

December 20-26

This Week

20 Sunday

21 Monday

22 Tuesday

23 Wednesday

24 Thursday

25 Friday

26 Saturday

Notes

top priorities for this week

_____
_____
_____
_____
_____

Victories for the week

looking ahead to next week

_____
_____
_____
_____
_____
_____
_____
_____

December 27-January 2

This Week

_____

_____

_____

_____

_____

_____

_____

_____

_____

_____

_____

_____

_____

_____

_____

_____

_____

_____

_____

_____

_____

_____

27 Sunday

28 Monday

29 Tuesday

30 Wednesday

31 Thursday

1 Friday

2 Saturday

Notes

top priorities for this week

_____

_____

_____

_____

_____

Victories for the week

looking ahead to next week

_____

_____

_____

_____

_____

_____

_____

_____

Notes

Notes

Notes

Made in the USA
Middletown, DE
16 July 2025